Bears

Bears

by Catherine Lukas

Reader's Digest

Published by The Reader's Digest Association Limited

London • New York • Sydney • Montreal

CONTENTS

Chapter 1

A bear cub grows up

DID YOU KNOW?

● Baby black bears usually weigh less than 500 grams at birth. Hold a 500g bag of sugar in your hand to get an idea of how little this is.

● Black bears like to lick sweet sap found underneath the outer layer of tree bark. The bears strip away the layer of bark with their teeth to get to the sapwood.

On a winter's night inside her den, Mother Bear gives birth to Baby Bear. He is as tiny as a kitten and has hardly any fur. He nuzzles against his mother's soft fur, drinking her warm milk.

For two months, snow falls outside. While Mother Bear sleeps, Baby Bear drinks, sleeps and grows. After four weeks, his eyes open and he has grown a covering of fur.

One day the bears are awakened by a steady dripping sound. The snow is melting. Baby Bear sniffs the warm spring air. Then he follows his mother out of the den. She moves slowly, as she has lost a lot of weight during the winter. It's time to eat.

Baby Bear watches his mother and quickly learns how to find food. He chews a stick, sniffing for ants and grubs to slurp up with his long, sticky tongue. He gobbles up sweet berries and nibbles on some wild flowers.

Mother Bear teaches him how to climb a tree. She knows he will be safe there while she hunts for food. The woods are full of dangers for little cubs. Wolves, mountain lions and grizzly bears sometimes hunt for little bears. Safe and sound high in the tree, Baby Bear nibbles on tasty leaves and takes a nap.

Suddenly Mother Bear rears up on her hind legs. She smells danger. She growls a warning and Baby Bear watches from his high perch.

It's a mountain lion! He stops when he sees Mother Bear towering over him, ready to fight, and scampers quickly away.

Little bears

Baby bears weigh 2 to 4 kilograms when they leave their den in the spring.

Bear beds

Many black bears prefer to sleep on soft beds for the winter rather than on bare cave floors. The bears build up their beds by bringing grass, leaves, moss and bark into their dens.

All summer and autumn, Mother Bear and her cub wander through the forests, eating as much as they can. She knows they must gain as much weight as possible to survive the coming winter. As the weather turns cold, Mother Bear searches for a new den in which they can spend the winter. At last she spots the perfect place – a cave with a narrow opening.

Mother Bear and her cub prepare the den by dragging in and laying down soft moss and leaves for their beds. Then they snuggle together and begin their long rest.

When spring arrives, Baby Bear is almost a fully grown black bear. He will stay with his mother for a little while longer, and then, as all bears do, he will wander off to a different part of the woods to begin his own bear adventures.

Chapter 2

The body of a bear

All bears shed their fur – called moulting – once a year when their new fur regrows thickly for the winter.

One rare kind of black bear has white or cream-coloured fur and lives off the coast of British Columbia in Canada. It is not a polar bear. Native Americans named these bears 'ghost bears.'

Which bear?

The two most common types of bears are black bears and brown bears. But it isn't always easy to tell the difference. Not all black bears are black, and not all brown bears are brown. Black bears can be black, bluish black, chocolate brown, reddish, cinnamon-coloured, tan or even white. Some have a white V or patch of white fur on their chest.

Brown bears are usually brown, but their fur colour can range from tan to black. Grizzly bear fur is light at the end of each hair, which makes the bears look 'grizzled' as if they are going grey. But it can still be difficult to tell other bears apart as the fur colour of young bears can change as they get older. For example, a black bear can have brown fur for a while. Also, the fur of some bears darkens with time.

So how do you tell the difference between black and brown bears? One way is by their size – brown bears are bigger and have a hump on their shoulders. Their ears are short, round and smaller than the ears of black bears. Brown-bear claws are longer and a lighter colour than those of black bears. Both black and brown bears live in the USA and Asia, but in Europe only brown bears live in the wild.

On the move

Bears look large and sluggish, but they can run as fast as 30 miles per hour for short distances. That's much faster than the fastest human sprinter.

While bears usually run and walk on all fours, they are able to stand upright on their back legs. They can walk in this position, but only for a few steps. Bears stand up to reach food, see into the distance, fight off an attacker or sniff something interesting in the air.

Bears spend a lot of time on the move, searching for food, a mate or a place to hibernate for the winter. They travel on remembered paths and will return to places that were good sources of food in the past. Bears will also explore new areas, especially when food is scarce.

DID YOU KNOW?

Bears are the most active in the early morning and evening. During the summer and early autumn, when they are storing up fat for their long winter's rest, bears may be active all day.

Despite their size, bears can run downhill, uphill and sideways.

Strong swimmers

Bears are good swimmers and like to be in the water. They go into the water to catch fish, cool off, escape irritating insects or an enemy, and sometimes just for fun. Polar bears are the best bear swimmers. They can swim continuously for hours. Black bears can swim a mile at a time without stopping.

DID YOU KNOW?

Bears' claws are curved, which makes these large animals surprisingly skilful. They use their claws to turn over rocks and logs, pick berries from bushes, catch fish and dig up roots to eat. The claws of black bears are so curved that they can even prise the lids off jars of food – as campers have discovered.

Just like people, bears are so-called 'plantigrades'. This means they walk by putting their entire foot flat on the ground, heel-first.

Sense of smell

Most bears have good eyesight and hearing but it's their sense of smell that is keenest. Bears can sniff out tiny insects inside logs or a dead animal a mile away. A bear's sense of smell is even better than that of a specially trained sniffer dog.

Bears also use their sense of smell to communicate with one another. They leave their scent on trees and bushes to 'tell' other bears they are in the area.

Tree-climbing

Black bears and European brown bears learn to climb trees when they are very young, and they soon discover how useful these plants are to them. Trees offer food (fruit, sweet sap and insects), safety from enemies and branches for resting or play. Some bears even hibernate in the crook of a thick branch for the whole winter!

Adult grizzly bears don't climb trees, because they are too big and heavy, but their cubs do.

A black bear climbs by digging into a tree trunk with its front paws and then pushing up with its hind legs, like a giant caterpillar. It comes down backwards, hind legs first, much like humans do, by shimmying down feet first. Bears also slide down tree trunks or jump from low branches.

Smart bears

Most bears are curious and quite intelligent. Bears will investigate new noises, smells and objects to see if they are edible or simply interesting to play with. They're even capable of outwitting humans who try to prevent them from finding food in dustbins and at campsites.

Bears also have very good memories. They can find their way to places where they have previously found food – even places they have visited only once before. They remember paths and routes they've walked in the past and the locations of favourite dens.

Bears make a range of noises, including grunting, blowing, woofing and growling. Cubs often whine or cry when they are upset or 'chuckle' when they are happy.

Chapter 3

Hungry as a bear

Although bears usually eat plants, they also love fish. Grizzlies are fond of salmon and wait beside rivers to catch them. When salmon are plentiful, brown bears may eat up to 40 kilograms a day.

DID YOU KNOW?

Black bears are not as clumsy as you might expect them to be. They can pick berries one at a time off bushes. They grasp and pull off the berries with their lips, which are very flexible. They also use their claws.

Lunchtime all the time

Although scientists classify bears as carnivores, meaning 'meat-eating' animals, bears are actually true omnivores — they eat both plants and animals. In fact, they tend to eat mostly plants. During the warm growing season, bears eat as much as 20 to 40 kilograms of food per day.

A black bear uses its long, sticky tongue to help it to collect tasty insects and to lap up sweet sap from the inner bark of trees. While most bears eat practically anything, their favourite foods are fruit, nuts, acorns, leaves, plants and insects. They also eat fish, small mammals and honey. In some areas, brown bears hunt larger animals such as moose, elk and mountain goats. What different bears eat can vary a great deal, depending on the region they live in and the time of the year.

Bears spend most of the spring, summer and autumn searching for food and eating in order to store as much fat as possible before they go to sleep for the winter — called hibernation.

Bear teeth

Bears have 42 teeth; humans have 32. A bear's teeth are shaped for eating both plants and animals. The pointed front teeth catch hold of food, such as a squiggly fish, while the bear's flat molars work just like yours for crushing and grinding.

Ready for winter

Bears are masters of survival – staying alive in difficult conditions. They have developed a perfect way to stay alive through long harsh winters, when food is scarce. Their trick is to stay asleep – or hibernate – so their bodies use much less energy.

Bears hibernate in dens, which they begin to get ready in September or October. Bears choose many different kinds of places to build their dens, including caves, holes in the ground or inside hollow logs. Sometimes they make their dens high up in a tree.

Some bears use the same den each winter. Others look for a new one every year.

During late summer and early autumn, bears know they have to gain as much weight as possible to get ready for the long winter. They eat as much as they can, day and night. Depending on the amount of food available, black bears at this time of year may gain 3 kilograms a day. The extra fat nourishes bears during the long winter and helps to keep them warm. As cold weather approaches, bears stop eating and grow more and more tired and sleepy.

Black bears living in Florida and other warm southern US states don't usually hibernate, although they often make a den and will sleep for periods of a few days during the winter. But, if a female black bear is pregnant, she will hibernate in the winter months.

Even though black bears and brown bears, like this grizzly, hibernate for the winter, they sometimes wake up and leave their dens for a little while to look for food in the snow.

During hibernation, a bear
lives off the food it has
stored inside its body.
A bear who sleeps through
the winter needs only
half the amount of oxygen
required when it's awake
and active.

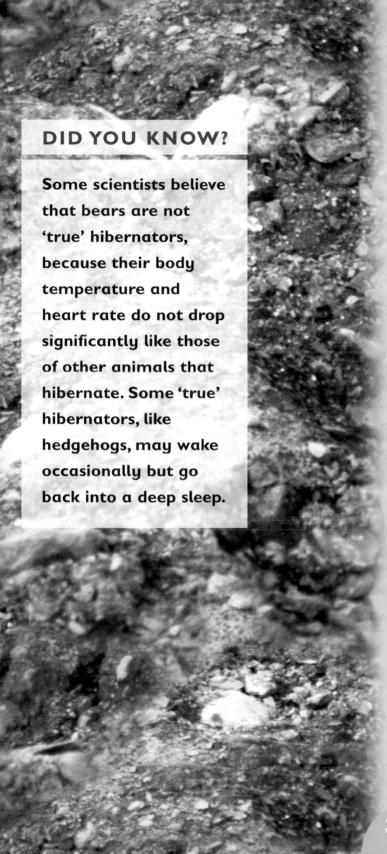

The big sleep

In cold climates, bears sleep in their dens for as long as seven months – usually from mid September to mid April. The colder the winter, the longer the bears sleep. They fall into a deep sleep and do not eat, drink, or get rid of waste materials during this time. Sometimes bears wake up and go out of their dens, but soon come back to carry on sleeping.

During hibernation, bears live off the body fat they have stored up before the winter. When the weather warms up, the bears leave their dens but they are often quite weak at first, as they lose as much as half their body weight while they sleep. As plants begin to grow again in the spring, the bears start to feed and gain weight and their energy returns.

DID YOU KNOW?

Some scientists believe that bears are not 'true' hibernators, because their body temperature and heart rate do not drop significantly like those of other animals that hibernate. Some 'true' hibernators, like hedgehogs, may wake occasionally but go back into a deep sleep.

Chapter 4

Bears and babies

Mother bears teach their cubs how to find food and how to escape from predators – other animals that could attack and eat them. They are fiercely protective of their little ones and will not hesitate to attack if their cubs are in danger.

Mother bears

Baby bears need their mums

At birth, baby bears are tiny, toothless and covered with wispy fur. They cannot see, hear, or smell until they are older. Baby bears are able to walk when they are five or six weeks old.

Female black bears and brown bears are ready to have babies when they are about five years of age. They give birth to cubs about every two or three years. Bears mate between May and July. But the baby bear does not begin to grow inside its mother until she has begun to hibernate, usually about November. Then its growth is fast — the bear cub is usually born in January or February, while the mother is hibernating. A mother bear generally gives birth to one to three cubs at a time, but scientists have recorded as many as six born to one mother. European brown bears often have twins.

Baby bears

When the mother bear gives birth to her cubs, she licks them and protects them by moving them next to her warm stomach. As soon as they begin to nurse, she falls back into her deep sleep. The cubs continue to eat and sleep for two to three more months. The mother bear's milk is very high in fat, and the babies grow quickly. When spring arrives, they weigh from 2 to 4 kilograms – about as much as a pet cat.

As soon as they emerge from their den, the mother bear teaches her cubs to find food. She shows them how to climb trees to avoid predators and, if necessary, rescues them from danger by carrying them gently in her mouth. In the autumn of the cubs' first year, both mother and cubs help prepare a den for the winter. They then sleep snuggled together for warmth until the spring.

Not long after the cubs leave the den for the second time, at about 17 months of age, they are ready to leave their mother. But she may recognise her offspring for many years to come and allow them to search for food in her territory.

DID YOU KNOW?

Bear cubs are very playful. They play with one another and their mother. They climb trees, wrestle, tackle, play fight, slide down hills and chase each other – all for fun. Playing is an important part of a bear's development. It helps to prepare cubs for the adult bear world by strengthening their physical skills. Playing also gives cubs the social skills they need to survive in the world. For example, by learning to understand other bears' behaviour, cubs will be prepared to know whether or not a strange bear is friendly.

Bear mums and cubs are very affectionate with each other. Bear cubs like to climb on their mum's back – for fun, comfort or to get a better view.

Chapter 5

Bears in the world

Polar bear cubs stay with
their mothers until they are
two years old.

Are koalas really bears?

Koalas look so much like teddy bears that many people refer to them as koala bears. But koalas are not really bears at all. They are members of a special group of mammals called marsupials.

Marsupial mums have a built-in pouch for carrying their babies. Can you think of another marsupial that has a pouch? If you thought of a kangaroo, you are right.

All kinds of bears

There are many kinds of bears that live in different places around the world.

Black bears and brown bears live in both North America and Asia. But only brown bears live in Europe.

Polar bears live where the climate is very cold – in the Arctic. They are the best swimmers of all the bears.

Spectacled bears get their name from the circles, which look like spectacles, around their eyes. These bears live in the Andes mountains of South America.

Sloth bears live in tropical and subtropical forests of India and Sri Lanka. They are slow movers.

Sun bears live in southeast Asian tropical and subtropical forests.

Panda bears live in China. They eat leaves from bamboo trees.

Bear homes

Black bears and brown bears mostly live in forests. Often a bear's territory is not one large area but several smaller ones linked by pathways. Within its home range, a bear can travel to different habitats – from mountainside to berry patches to rivers with salmon.

FAST FACTS ABOUT BEARS

SCIENTIFIC NAME	Black bear Grizzly bear Eurasian brown bear	*Ursus Americanus* *Ursus arctos horribilis* *Ursus arctos arctos*
ORDER	Carnivora	
FAMILY	Ursidae	
SIZE	Black bears Grizzly bears Eurasian brown bear	Up to 2m in length 2m to 2.5m in length 1.5m to 2.8m in length
WEIGHT	Black bears Grizzly bears Eurasian brown bear	Males average 130kg Females average 68kg Males from 180–360kg Females from 130–180kg Males from 135–320kg Females from 100–200kg
LIFE SPAN	Black bears Grizzly bears Eurasian brown bears	Up to 32 years in the wild 25–30 years in the wild 25–36 years in the wild
HABITAT	Black bears Grizzly bears Eurasian brown bears	Forests, woodlands, swamps Mountain forests, tundra Forests, alpine areas, tundra

Future of bears

Black bears and brown bears are not endangered but other bears are at risk, especially giant pandas. The habitats of all bears are continually being threatened or shrunk by expanding human populations. The Arctic, where polar bears live, is in danger because of global warming.

The most important way
to protect bears is by
protecting and preserving
their habitat so that the
bears have plenty of room
in which to roam.

GLOSSARY OF Wild WORDS

blubber	a thick layer of fat under the skin that keeps an animal warm and helps it to float
carnivore	a meat-eating animal
cub	a very young bear
den	a place where a wild animal rests or sleeps
edible	safe to eat as food
endangered	a species (a specific type) of plant or animal in danger of extinction
global warming	a rise in the average temperature of the Earth's atmosphere
habitat	the natural environment where a plant or animal lives
hibernate	to go into a deep sleep all winter
mammal	an animal with a backbone and hair on its body that drinks milk from its mother when it is born
marsupial	a kind of mammal whose mother carries her babies in a pouch
molars	big teeth in the back of the mouth used for grinding food
moult	to shed old fur, hair, or skin and regrow new fur, hair or skin

moss	a small green plant that forms a soft mat on moist ground, rocks, or trees	protein	a substance found in all animals that is needed for growth and life
nourish	to supply with food and moisture, helping a creature to stay alive	scent	a smell left by an animal that other animals can identify
nurse	to feed a baby animal with milk from the mother's breast	tundra	a large plain in the Arctic with no trees
offspring	young animals that have the same mother		
omnivore	an animal that eats both plants and meat		
predator	an animal that hunts and eats other animals to survive		

INDEX

CREDITS

Bears is an *All About Animals* fact book
published by The Reader's Digest Association Limited

Written by Catherine Lukas

Copyright © 2005 The Reader's Digest Association, Inc.
This edition was adapted and published in 2008 by
The Reader's Digest Association Limited
11 Westferry Circus, Canary Wharf, London E14 4HE
Reprinted in 2010

Editor: Rachel Warren Chadd
Designer: Nicola Liddiard
Art editor: Simon Webb

We are committed both to the quality of our products and the service we provide
to our customers. We value your comments, so please do contact us on
08705 113366 or via our website at www.readersdigest.co.uk

If you have any comments or suggestions about the content of our books,
email us at gbeditorial@readersdigest.co.uk

Printed in China

ISBN: 978 0 276 44319 0
Book code: 640-002 UP0000-2
Oracle code: 504500008H.00.24